T0158905

POSITIVE POWER & HAPPINESS!™

POSITIVE POWER & HAPPINESS!™

PP&HITM EMPOWERING YOURSELF INTO A JOYFUL & HAPPY LIFE!

CAROLYN A. W. VAN RAVENHORST

POSITIVE POWER & HAPPINESS!™
PP&H!™ EMPOWERING YOURSELF INTO
A JOYFUL & HAPPY LIFE!

iUniverse books may be ordered through booksellers or by contacting:

iUniverse
1663 Liberty Drive
Bloomington, IN 47403
www.iuniverse.com
1-800-Authors (1-800-288-4677)

ISBN: 978-1-5320-0654-8 (sc)
ISBN: 978-1-5320-0653-1 (e)

Library of Congress Control Number: 2016914525

Print information available on the last page.

iUniverse rev. date: 12/10/2016

CONTENTS

Introduction

INTRODUCTION

Welcome to the workbook Positive Power & Happiness!™

First I like to introduce myself to you to and give you the main reason why I wrote this book.

I am Carolyn van Ravenhorst and I am a Business Consultant, Turn Around Manager and Entrepreneur, Real Estate Investor, Film maker, World wide traveler, People & Life Lover. My hobbies are Singing, Entertaining and Acting.

During my business career many people asked me "my secret".

Why I am so happy, powerful, full of life & positive drive, radiant, energetic and successful!

Some told me that -even when I managed complex leadership reorganization projects - I looked self-assured, happy, relaxed, confident and I was humoristic. Even during this work I seemed to be always in a driven 'sun shining holiday' mood. However, I changed organizations successfully and doubled the profit fast. As a bonus, I changed the whole work culture into a positive, powerful, renewed motivated and happy culture.

Sometimes unexpectedly, I bumped to people in a restaurant, somewhere in the street or at the beach and I got always great and interesting conversations.

For them, they told me, I was there at the right time at the right moment. Sometimes I had just a very short positive word or a humoristic act to them and we had great fun!

I inspired them and made their day! And after taking some more time for these unexpected meetings -strange enough- I got always lots of extra time in my busy schedule.

A good friend of mine, for whom I did a re-organizing job in his company, asked me: "Carolyn, please write a book to explain your secrets of how everybody can experience a good, powerful & happy life". "The world needs this"!

Not only from him, but I got really many many questions about what my secrets were for having such a good life. And too many people asked me to write a book about this 'powerful secret" of my life.

Because of all curiosity of all the contacts I made during my worldwide travels and businesses, I finally made the decision to start writing my book about the Positive Power & Happiness!™ Life Style.

"I am always focussed on my own happy, busy life and clear goals and I never compare myself with others. I use my Power to develop all my great given talent"

"More and more I see people struggle, being unhappy and getting lost in life."

My mission is to finish this book TODAY. Therefore It is not a perfect book, but its finally there. For you".

The crucial question in my book will be "Why is it important to be just you, as who you really are?"

Being you - as you really are- living the life of your true authentic self is VERY important. Let me explain this to you before we start with the **5 PP&H! Entertrainments** in the next Chapters..

Living and making choices conform your authentic self, is not that easy as we think it is. It needs lots of Positive Power and strong developed characteristics.

We live in a world full of expectations. We are controlled by media, fashion, habits, family traditions, religion and by rules made by our communities, governments and the country and cultures we grew up and live(d) in.

When we grew up, our parents did their very best to educate us being at least a decent child. We grew up as a person who learnt to *repress a lot of natural behaviors, spontaneous acts* as very natural loving beings. Some children even *were teached to gain unnatural behaviors and therefore expected to choose a direction they even were not interested in at ALL.*

In small families is more control and a "feeling" that we have to educate more than necessary to children.

Well, be relaxed. Most children are clever enough and always find their way in life and really know by themselves what they really want.

Children are not born insecure. Insecurities comes up by too much controlling and by unfair rules or unspoken behavior by communities. Of course there must be some average boundaries, but in only a fair way in my opinion. More about this in my next book :)

This influence, also in greater surroundings as social communities, schools, university, work area etc.. brings us to a level of UNNatural -or even worse- repressed and controlled behavior.

In case of childhood; If you do and act as expected by your surroundings, you are labeled as a good child..

If you have as a kid a very strong character and personality - in best case scenario - you can escape these kind of unnatural strong influences around you. Or you will at least be labeled as "complicated" "black sheep" "hard to handle" or "rebel". In worst case scenario you even got punished or abused.

In most cases these influences can lead in older ages into an insecure behavior, which is not you anymore as an authentic human, but your unnatural self!

That's why most mature people are looking for their whole life to get back their real happy authentic self again. With help of therapists or alone. But most of them look to far. Outside them. Getting "kicks". Fur-fill their lives with outside actions. But never find real balance or get sustainable peace in their soul.

In general you see that the people around you, want you to be "a social acceptable" person. Happy or not. They don't care as long as you are socially adjusted by them. It is a conflicting way of life for many. But as "mature people' we learned to suppress this.

This is why the therapists are never out of work. They can't solve these suppressed society problems and really don't know how to help their clients to be happy again. It is a proven fact that suppressed feelings and emotions causes depression!!

In the psychological work field they found in the meantime a lot of labels for all different and *not social* accepted behaviors of people. And of course the chemical industries live from all the great repeated medicines they found for all these 'diseases'... And makes millions, billions of profit, but of course not to make you really Happy and Healthy.

In the meantime all these "patients" believe there is no hope for them and accepted their lethargic state of life.. With continuous (life long?) talks with therapists and taking these medicines. Of course with not any result or a healthy receipt to a real happy life. They just like to keep each other busy. But they make at least money. And the "patients" are getting nothing back in return.

Who is here the problem? These unique authentic persons, who got lost and sick by these intolerable society's? Or the social medical area's who are not able or equipped to handle differences in our social environment, cultures and communities? Think for yourself.

Some are teached by parents, teachers and families to be kind, if we had to be UNkind. Friendly, were we must to be UNfriendly.. We adjusted ourselves in an UNhealthy way to all people around us.

That is were the stress and inner conflicts with our real authentic self all starts.

Worst case scenario; You are gonna live your entire life as someone else and you are only very busy to fulfill others expectations, society and keeping on pleasing others.

What a busy job. And exhausting. And what a mental prison. Depressing. To just keep others Happy. Not being the real authentic person as you are meant to be.

"In this book I will teach you how you can look at your life in a very clear perspective. And how you can acquire for yourself a sustainable Happy Life."

With my 5 PP&H! Entertrainments I will teach you how to change your life step by step, into your own unique Positive Power & HappinessTM! Life Style.

These 5 PP&H! Entertrainments are mentioned to bright up your vision about your beautiful gift, called life. It will help and teach you to make a great and positive impact in your own personal life and the ones around you!

I give Great Thanks and Honor to our Loving Creator, who is the Greatest and Humoristic (!) Inspirator of sustainable unconditional Powerful love for ALL of us!

I am convinced and urged by this Higher Power to finally write this book NOW. And I wrote it. For you.

Thank you.

With LOVE,
Carolyn

CHAPTER 1

BASICS

The life you get on Earth is a tiny and short time you get. We have a privilege to be here. Your life is very unique. You have specific talents and gifts for a very important reason.

'This life cannot effect you negative at all, unless you actively allow this negative Power in your brains'

The power of your brains determines the quality of your life. Your brains are the stirring wheel of your life direction. And only you have the choice to use your negative Power or your Positive Power about happenings in your life. As a consequence you will feel yourself miserable or happy.

Only you can make the choice about the direction of your life. And only you decide what the following negative or just positive feelings will be about this choice. That is where this workbook is all about.

In this workbook I will teach The 5 Positive Power & Happiness! Entertrainments (PP&H!E)

The last empty pages in this book are meant to make notes and to write down your progression each day, week and month until you "get' it!

This PP&H!E will help you to be very Joyful, Successful and Powerful. Every day. Every moment. In any circumstances. And gaining the awareness that your life is all about Positive Powerful choices.

And as a bonus and result you will feel Positive Powerful & Happy!

I guarantee that these 5 Powerful PP&H!E will transform your life, into a life that will make a Positive Powerful & Inspiring impact on yourself and others.

I will go straight to the point, but first I like to share a background story about my general experiences with people I met.

I experienced that every single person has his or her own Life story.. If I asked them what or how they are doing, you hear a lot of different stories.. Mostly I hear this kind of reaction: Well I have a good job and nice life and family but....

"Listen *what happened to me...*" And their life story begins.

"What happened to me" is mostly a start off of a victim mentality.

Life seemed to be not fair to them.

Life can effect us in a way we *can feel* overwhelmed and we can *feel as* a victim. But feeling like a victim may be temporary and that feeling is ok for a very good reason; This does not mean you have to STAY in life as a victim.

In this work book I guide you to get control over your thoughts and over your life.

In this book I teach you: "How you can get out of this victim state as fast as you can!" It all starts with your thoughts. In the following chapters I teach you step by step how to do this fast. Repeating my PP&H! Entertrainments until you 'get' it, will help you to integrate this training in your personality and as a part of your new identity.

Only if you like to walk backwards, walk as a victim in an sustainable unhappy life.. Please do not read this book.

I challenge you to practice these 5 PP&H ENTERTRAINMENTS in the next chapters and motivate you to transform your life totally!!

I believe in you.

You are Powerful.

You can do it!!

CHAPTER 2

PP&H! **ENTERTRAINMENT 1**

YOUR INNER CHILD

Entertrainment 1
To integrate a Positive Powerful & Happy life into your life right now, I introduce you to start with the first very important basic training.

Take some time for yourself, sitting in a comfortable (hairy :) chair in a quiet place.. or your favorite spot somewhere in nature.

Ask yourself the following questions:

What is most important for me right now?

Think about this for a moment. Listen to your heart.

It can be Love, Succes, Being healthy, Being good to Family and Friends, or having lots of Holidays or Traveling, Being Famous, Being happy, Dancing, Singing and so on. Try to be specific to yourself.

Close your eyes. Breath slowly. Relax.

Go actively back in time with your thoughts to the age of the 4, 5 years old kid you was...

Think about your childhood period for at least 10 minutes with the awareness of what your feelings are. Dream away back into that time.

Open your eyes.

Breath slowly and just relax..

Then ask yourself these questions about your childhood;

1) How did I feel?
2) What did I do?
3) What made me happy?
4) What was important to me?
5) What kinda fantasies did I have as a kid.. Do I remember..?
6) Do I still have these fantasies?
7) What can I teach myself about this information?
8) What do I like to do now?

"I just imagine. I will have no limited thoughts. Only imaginations, imaginations and imaginations"...

Take your time, dream away and get that relaxed state of just being a "being'. In the now. With the imagination of being that kid again..

Take your time to dream and imagine about the life you love. Do not limit yourself with your thoughts. Just dream away. Everything is possible.

Ok. You have answers.. Weird? Surprising? Or just fun?!

Declare to yourself: "***I realize that today I have a new choice. I take actions to develop step by step to live the life I really want. I like to take actions to what truly makes me happy***". Repeat and declare this words frequently to yourself in a daily affirmation.

Write the answers down in the last blanc pages of this workbook.

When you repeat this training, you can eventually see different outcomes. That's cool. It is all an insight about the real you.

CONCLUSION

The very important reason of this first Entertrainment is;

To challenge yourself to accept fully, at least "allow"... in your mind and feelings, your inner child again. That kid that still desperately seeks, screams and really needs you TODAY and in the now! And to fully allow yourself that you always have the choice to act and feel as that child again.. Free, Happy, Dreaming, Fantasying etc. I hope with this workbook to make you aware that your inner child is still a very important part IN you.

And that you will fully allow this inner child again and to integrate her or himself in your life again. Introduce yourself to your inner child again and simply say out loud:

"Hi mature woman or man"! "I am here with AND for you to fully support you in your mature life and to be really one with you again"

Then take the chance & 100% motivation to work from this point of a renewed insight of your real authentic self.

Step by step as if you learn to walk again...

If you practice this first training every day, I am convinced - that you will embrace your little child again.. and that you will feel really happy, loved and accepted. By yourself. Only you can do this.

Try to let this feeling sink down in your soul.

Well... sound easy ah..? It is very easy, if you practice this so frequently until you know deep down in your soul, that you already fully embraced your inner child. Soon you will be more and more aware of yourself as a real happy person.

Because you found your the real authentic YOU.

My advice is to do this PP&H! Entertrainment intensively at least 30 minutes a day during the first 4 weeks. Then I advice you to do this training at least 3 times a week for at least 3 months.

CHAPTER 3

PP&H! **ENTERTRAINMENT 2**

INTEGRATE YOUR INNER CHILD IN YOUR MATURE PERSONALITY

This Entertrainment 2 is to help you to actively integrate (ground!) your inner child into your mature personality today. The goal is to truly realize that your inner child is of great help to support and empower your personality.

It helps you to be your true authentic self and to feel fully loved and accepted by yourself. No fake or adjusted attitude is needed. It's you.

As a bonus you will find back that funny play-full natural kid inside of you.

'The Positive Challenge in this Entertrainment 2 is to sustain your renewed transformed personality and to explore with this new experience in new various and creative ways!!'

All you need to learn is to simply *allow, love and fully embrace your inner child.* Loved and recognized by yourself. Happily welcomed and integrated into your mature life now. From this renewed point of view you will automatically see in a more clear way the direction in life you like to go. And what kind of actions you need to make to live your life Authentically, Joyful, Powerful and Happy. Finally only YOU will know how to live the life that supports your real authentic YOU!

After doing this Entertraining very well, you feel at home and peaceful within, fully embraced and loved by yourself. You made peace with your self (soul) and accepted and fully love yourself as who you truly are..!!

There we go!

PP&H! Entertrainment 2

Look for a relaxed place somewhere, or go and sit into your comfortable (hairy :) chair again. Be sure you have space around you (quiet nature, beach is very good too) A place were you not feel distracted and where you feel free and safe.

In my workshops and seminars I experience this always as a very funny and entertaining training. Especially because you do this with others around you. But it's fun to do this by yourself too.

Are you ready?

Think and dream about the most hilarious, crazy, surrealistic film where you will have a leading role... Your film. It's all perfect wherever you dream or imagine about. Make it only your imagination; Just light, hilarious and very fun. If you start laughing about yourself you do this training good :) If you start out laughing about yourself until your belly hurts.. You do this training excellent!!! Laugh and if you can.. cry out loud in tears from laughing about your hilarious imaginations.

Imagine so extremely funny and out of the box, until you feel fully free to even BE that happy kid! It doesn't matter if you think the most crazy, ugly, funny, stupid things: If it all makes you happy.. It's ok! It's you. Just you, your imaginations and your inner child having fun.

Then ask yourself these questions:

1) How did I feel?
2) What did I do ?
3) What made me Happy?
4) What was important to me?
5) What kind of fantasies came up?

6) What kind of positive actions can I take, to start my new Positive Power & Happiness!™ Life Style?

"I realize that I have a free choice, to do what I really want in life and I will take serious steps to do it! Forgetting ego and expectations of others. I will just do it for me and act on it!"

You will feel free, light and happy. I guarantee you with a big smile!!

Write the new insights about yourself in the special PP&H!™ blanco work pages of this book. You can also buy yourself a nice colored (happy) notebook and save this book for your personal & private PP&H!™ Life Style notes.

CONCLUSION

Entertrainment 1 gave you a basic, but very important training finding your inner child, were you can go from to support your real authentic self.

You learned to embrace & love your inner child again.

In Entertrainment 2 you learned to integrate & balance your inner child with your mature personality.

It is the best combination of the real authentic you.

If you do this Entertraining 1 and 2 frequently and well, I challenge you to present your renewed authentic personality to yourself and the world around you, without any shame or hesitation. It's YOU.

"A child feels naturally happy, free. A child comes on this earth with natural trust in life & people. A

child lives in the moment, don't need a lot of stuff, is creative, knows intuitively very well what he or she want or not want; like or do not like. There is no need for distractions from media or any other outside influences."

What is here the secret? You basically feel that you don't need a lot, to be really happy in life. And that there is a lot stuff and ballast your soul don't need at ALL.

Teach yourself daily to listen to your real inner self.

It is to support and love yourself. This is not egoistic. It's saving your life from lots of troubles and disappointments, unnecessary hurts, failures and time assuming wrong directions. If you do and practiced Entertrainment 1 and 2 very well, you can go straight forward to the Entertrainment 3 in my next chapter.

You already made the strong foundation for starting your Positive & Powerful & Happiness!™ Life Style!

Advice is to do Entertraining 2 at least 3 times a week for 30 minutes in the first Month. Then slow down to a minimum of 1 time a week for 3 Months.

CHAPTER 4

PP&H! **ENTERTRAINMENT 3**

SUPPORT YOUR AUTHENTIC SELF

In this Entertrainment 3, I will teach you to sustain your inner Happiness day by day, moment by moment.

I teach you in my Entertrainments to be aware in thinking the right thing in an entertaining and humoristic way. It gives you - when you get used to this- tons of fun and it is instantly very effective!!

Changing negative thinking -we call this TT, Trash Thinking- must be immediately banned for good out of your total system. Then activate your new habit by Retraining your Brain from Negative Thoughts into Positive thoughts.

Your actions, feelings, mood will change automatically into a very Positive, Powerful and

Happy Life, despite your circumstances at that very moment..!

"It is not the problem that is the problem, but It's the way how you look at the problem, that's the problem.." (JOHNNY DEPP)

I give you the tools you need to own this Positive Power and how to step out of your comfort zone, take action to get the results of this Powerful & Happy life you deserve!

From now on you take control, gain successes and own that Positive Powerful Life every moment & every day!

PP&H! Entertrainment 3:
1. Start doing daily *at least* 2 new things, what you really like and what makes you happy... and you live already in a starting flow of Positivity.
2. If you have a life partner; End every day with asking each other the 10 positive happenings of that day. This will help you having a happy feeling at the end of every day. If you live by yourself just write or say out loud the 10 positive happenings of your day. Make it fun & joy-able!
3. Start every morning with compliments to yourself. In front of the mirror makes it more

real and fun. Look at yourself and say loud to yourself at least 3 compliments about your appearance, 3 about your character and 3 about your qualities, 3 about your competences.. Repeat that as must as you like. If you get used to this Entertraining then make it more fun to say this in a melody or in your (funny) favorite song.

Important for this training is: Make it very fun & light. It will make your day!

4. During the day; Retrain your brain immediately from negative thoughts into positive thoughts. As soon as you feel something coming up in your brains, that makes you feel sad or unhappy.. even for a little moment.. be aware of what you just was thinking.. then go immediately from that 1 Negative thought to at east 3 (!) Positive thoughts.

   If you get used to this training, you will only allow positive and happy thoughts. As a result you feel yourself a positive and happy person.

"Know that only you have control about how you think and how you decide to feel."

It's a choice only YOU can make by a daily training and practicing of these PP&H! Entertrainments. Train yourself so much until you control this as a

TOP Sport! Make it fun, joyful and humorous, until you are so used to it and do it all automatically.

It is like learning to fly in a Plane. At first you just see all the buttons in the cockpit. You can even panic. But if you learn to trust your knowledge and get fully aware, you trained yourself to fly on the automatic Pilot of the Positive Power flow & Happiness!™ Life Style!

CHAPTER 5

PP&H! **ENTERTRAINMENT 4**

RELATIVATION

VALUES

VISION

PP&H! Entertrainment 4
Make notes how you think you can relativate life.

Is that for humor of you?

Using Humor can be a very Powerful tool to relativate any (unexpected) stressful circumstance or situation in your life.

Think about what you can add in your life as your unique relativation tool..

If you find the right tool: It makes you immediately feel good.

Use your tool from now on in your daily life.

Make notes about your life vision.

Make notes about your values.

Make notes about how you can make your life 100% in line with your values & life vision.

Do this Entertrainment 3 times a week for 30 minutes.

Outcomes may vary. Write it all down.

After doing this 3 times a week during 30 minutes and for at least 2 Months, you know your Relativation tools, Values and Life Vision.

CONCLUSION

*Here you have the secret of all the people who live already a Positive Powerful, Happy, Balanced and Successful life! * They know how to relativate Life and they strongly know their Values and Life Vision.*

And they go actively after their goals, with all their Positivity and inner Power to reach these goals and focus only what makes them Happy & Successful in Life.

Nobody can motivate you into a Positive Powerful & Happy Life Style. Only you give yourself that permission.

"If you give full Power back to yourself, you allow yourself to live your authentic Positive Powerful & Happy Life!!"

If you train *yourself to be aware of your strong inner Positive Power and know what you want and like to do with your life, you simply go after it. You seek for people with the SAME purpose, values, vision and goals.*

This is the indispensable POSITIVE POWERFUL SPIRIT and required to get huge & guaranteed success* & a fur filled and happy life!!

In Companies it is very important to select 100% motivated and equipped employees. They must clearly know their tasks. They must have creativity and get realistic, feasible timetables to reach the clear company goals to get the right results in the right time. That's how success is gained.

————The best motivated marketeers and promoters of your Company are the Employees who are already convinced by them selves that the values, vision, strategy and Company Goals are the same as their own————-

For the Managers, Directors and CEO's who are reading my book: You already know that it is very important to be clear and upfront to all your employees and teach them your Company Statements, Values, Vision and Goals. This and much more customized advises (!) will give your company guaranteed 100% succes!! It will go way to far to write all these strict and customized success advices in this book.

You deserve SUCCES*.

You deserve HAPPINESS in work and private life.

You deserve to HAVE POSITIVE POWER to go into the RIGHT direction of our life desires!

* With Success I mean developing your Talent, Work,Business, being Happy, having Good Life experiences, Traveling, Loved and being Love etc. Even If you are ill, disabled or in other bad circumstances: It's about dealing with life in a Balanced, Positive Powerful and Happy way.

* Chasing Material things are temporary and absolutely not a guarantee to get a Happy Fulfilled Life!

CHAPTER 6

PP&H! **ENTERTRAINMENT 5**

DIRECTION & GOALS

Entertrainment 5
Go to your favorite quiet spot in nature or just relax in your chair.

Imagine and think about yourself were you like to be in 3 years (goals).

Make notes.

Then think about steps you need to take (direction).

Make your Clear Goals for:

    Year 1
    Year 2
    Year 3

Ask yourself these questions:

WHAT TIME do I need by every step per year?

Write this down.

WHAT ACTIONS do I need by every step per year?

Write this down.

Use the K.I.S.S. Method. Keep It Short & Simple.

"Play" around with this Entertrainment. You don't need to have right answers immediately.

Do this Entertrainment 3 times a week for at least 30 minutes.

You need 3 Months for training.

No hurry.

Take time to let all this new knowledge about yourself easily sink down into your soul.

Be sure that this Training keeps you Positive, Motivated, Inspired and Happy.

Keep it fun and 'light". Until you are sure about your Goals and Direction.

Go back to Entertrainment 1 and 2.

See if it is still in alignment with your soul!

CONCLUSION

This last Entertrainment is mentioned to motivate you into your renewed Positive Power & Happiness!™ Life Style. YOU only can do this!

Take control over your Life and own this new Life Style. You deserve to be Happy, Successful and Goal driven!

You tapped into your strong and available Positive Power.

Only act conform your true authentic self to love & support yourself..... and thereafter act on what makes you Happy!

The Butterfly example
Being in a state of sustainable happiness at heart, looks like a butterfly who comes out of his or her cocon.

The world around, the society, media or circumstances have- without your full awareness- spinned this cocon around you...And let you believe what is going to make you Happy.

As a puber you possibly fighted against all given standards and rules. That's a very healthy part of growing up. Some people like to be that rebel their whole entire life. Because they still can't stand this 'unnatural cocon' which the world around them is constantly spinning this around them.

"A Butterfly only wants to fly and show off its beautiful colors and live their life fully!! That's what the Purpose of this butterfly is!"

But sadly and finally most people accept the average depressing 'prison' they live (or better die) in. The butterfly let his wings down and don't took the change to show off.

Circumstances, like illness, sad experiences of life, disability, death of loved ones, being rejected, feeling not loved, respected or accepted, not getting the right job, whatever happens etc etc..: All these happenings in your life can wind that invisible cloth around you... slowly... but surely... and over the years... without your awareness you live in the prison of a life you don't want or fit in!

Until you finally get lost in darkness and depression. You just lost.. yourself. The only one and very unique masterpiece on the Planet is: The Powerful YOU.

But you lost yourself in a unhappy & unfulfilled Life.

Which can lead into bad habits and worse, addictions; like overuse of drugs or alcohol etc. to cover your inner pain and suffering deep inside and so on...

BUT.... I am very happy that you trained yourself the 5 basic Entertrainments in this workbook, to find your real authentic self again.

Some people still believe they can find it by only changing their circumstances. Then they realize in a later stage, they are still lost in traps of other people and want to change again and again.

And they still feel alone deep inside of their soul. Because they forgot to start at first to love and embrace their own precious soul and meaning of their life..

CHAPTER 7

NEW DIRECTION & PURPOSE

After doing the 5 Entertrainments in this workbook very well, you now own that Positive Power, Joy and Happiness in your soul. Congrats! You did it!!

You made the choice to direct your Life with all your Power into a total new Direction to support your authentic self.

You made a Positive & Powerful change!!

To keep that feeling of returning "home" and "finding yourself back" you must continue to practice these 5 Entertrainments, until it is a natural part of your personality.

Your new state of mind will give you Joy, Light, Happiness, and Gratefulness.

You are in alignment with your soul again. As a direct result you came in alignment with your

33

Creator too. You get the tools in hands to live your life Happily and with great Purpose.

The Creator of the Universe gives you the great gift of Power and Positivity to develop your unique & great given talents.

You are a masterpiece. Unique and handmade by your Creator. You are loved. He created you and the Earth wonderful. As a perfect match. For you.. Think about this for a moment. You have a huge privileged to be here - only temporary - in a responsible way on this Planet Earth.

You and your Creator are one and are meant to work together in Inspiring & Creative ways. That is a Purpose. The deep knowledge that you are connected in your soul with your Creator feels "at home". You both are one. The Creator and the Creation belongs together. If this connection is broken and unhealed, humans feel lost.

Eternal love for you was always there and will be always there. This love is for free, unconditional and eternal. This love will never go away from you. You feel and know this, as you are in touch with your real authentic self, your soul.

Even if you don't feel this, that love is still there. Your Creator don't expect anything in return.

Just receive this gift of love, peace and happiness today in your heart. And receive as a direct result pure Joy and Happiness!!

Michael Jacksons song was: "We are the ones, we are the children.."

We are all Family from the beginning. We are united. We are one.

His very beloved children in this world are made perfectly. They have the privilege to live temporary at Planet Earth, our visible world. But their souls will live eternal and will always be connected with Powerful Inspiration of their Creator. Tap from now on into that Inspiring Positive Power!! It's yours!!

It's a great you trained yourself the 5 PP&H! Entertrainments.

Now I challenge you to fully tap into your renewed insights and go 100% for the Positive Power & Happiness!™ Life Style!!

"If everyone finds back peace in their soul, there are no conflicts anymore and life will be Positive, Powerful & Happy!!"

Much Love!!
Carolyn

NOTES

NOTES

NOTES

NOTES

NOTES

NOTES

NOTES

NOTES

NOTES

NOTES

NOTES

NOTES

NOTES

NOTES

NOTES

NOTES

NOTES

NOTES

NOTES

NOTES

NOTES

NOTES

NOTES

NOTES

NOTES

NOTES

NOTES

NOTES

NOTES

NOTES

NOTES

NOTES

NOTES

NOTES

NOTES

NOTES

NOTES

NOTES

NOTES

NOTES

NOTES

NOTES

NOTES

NOTES

NOTES

NOTES

NOTES

NOTES

NOTES

NOTES

NOTES

NOTES

NOTES

NOTES

NOTES

NOTES

NOTES

NOTES

NOTES

NOTES

NOTES

NOTES

NOTES

NOTES

NOTES

NOTES

NOTES

NOTES

Printed in the United States
By Bookmasters